Rhyming Words workbook

This cheese belongs to

_____

Rhyming Words workbook

This crease belongs to

Table of Contents

Color the Space

Directions: Color the spaces that rhyme with the object in the middle section

Color the Space

Directions: Color the spaces that rhyme with the object in the middle section

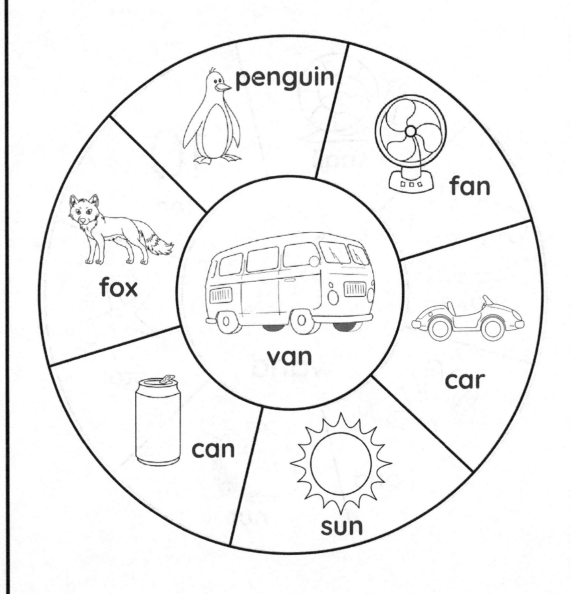

Color the Space

Directions: Color the spaces that rhyme with the object in the middle section

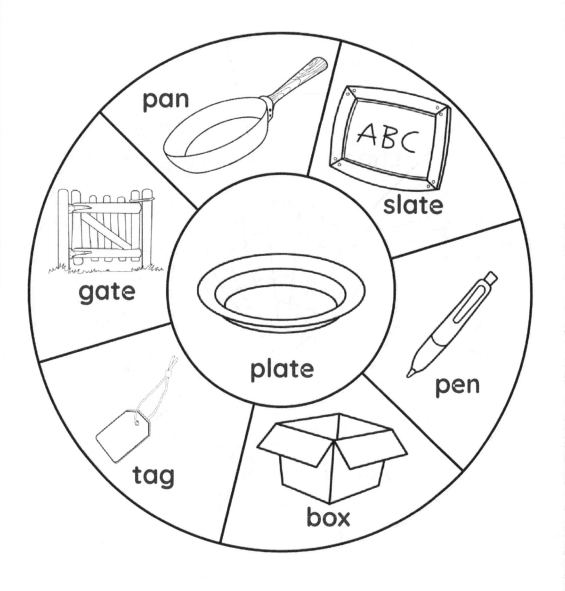

Color the Space

Directions: Color the spaces that rhyme with the object in the middle section

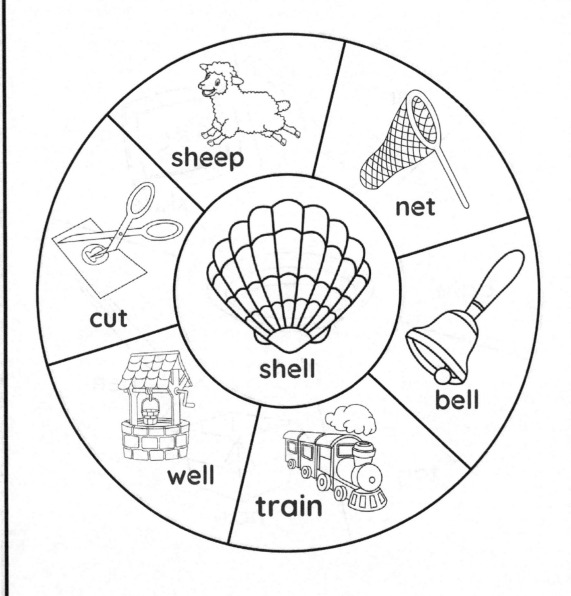

Color the Space

Directions: Color the spaces that rhyme with the object in the middle section

Color the Space

Directions: Color the spaces that rhyme with the object in the middle section

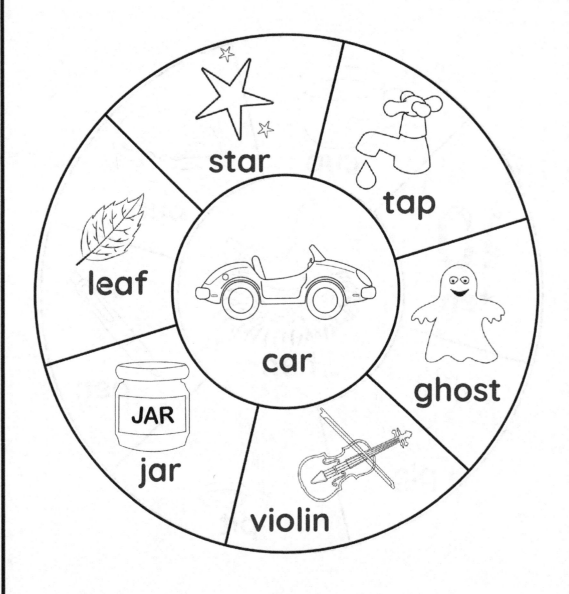

Color the Space

Directions: Color the spaces that rhyme with the object in the middle section

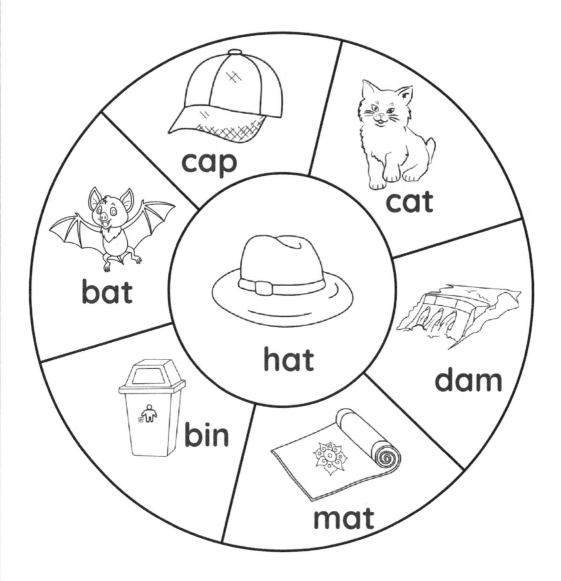

Draw a line to match the pictures

Directions: Draw a line between the words that rhymes

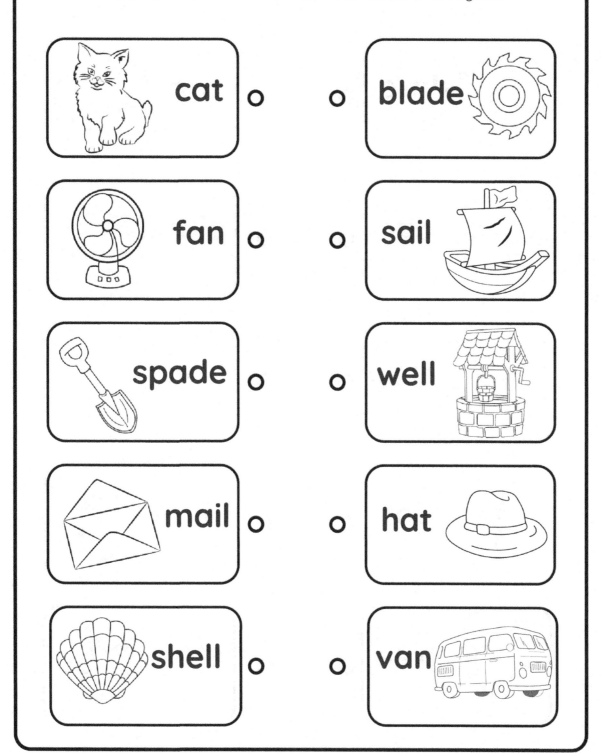

cat   blade

fan   sail

spade   well

mail   hat

shell   van

Draw a line to match the pictures

Directions: Draw a line between the words that rhymes

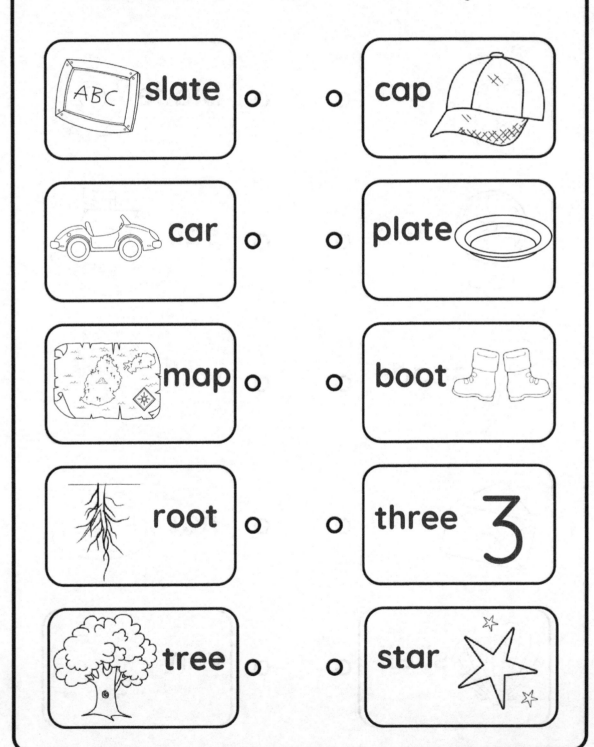

slate ○ ○ cap

car ○ ○ plate

map ○ ○ boot

root ○ ○ three 3

tree ○ ○ star

Draw a line to match the pictures

Directions: Draw a line between the words that rhymes

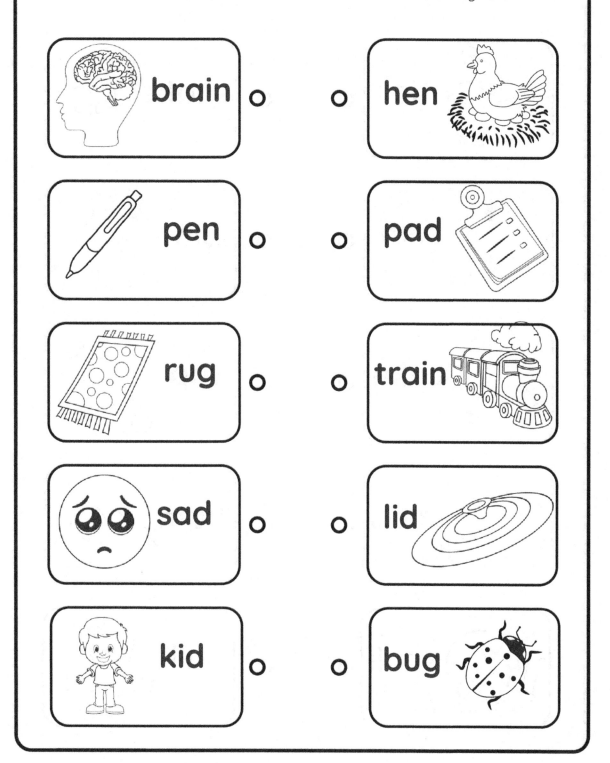

brain o   o hen

pen o   o pad

rug o   o train

sad o   o lid

kid o   o bug

Draw a line to match the pictures

Directions: Draw a line between the words that rhymes

tin ○   ○ snake

ram ○   ○ bin

cake ○   ○ tap

map ○   ○ ham

snail ○   ○ sail

Circle pictures that rhymes

Directions: Circle one picture in each row that rhymes with the first
One in the box

mug	snail	bug	fan
hen	cup	book	ten
sun	bun	moon	cake
pig	gate	lamp	wig
pin	train	tin	pen

Circle pictures that rhymes

Directions: Circle one picture in each row that rhymes with the first One in the box

dog	van	brain	frog
toy	cap	boy	nest
fox	box	net	star
well	moon	bell	pot
crab	snail	ham	cab

Circle pictures that rhymes

Directions: Circle one picture in each row that rhymes with the first
One in the box

train	jar	plate	brain
dam	ham	mat	jet
pot	bag	dot	pad
can	pan	car	cake
lip	cow	pen	tulip

Circle pictures that rhymes

Directions: Circle one picture in each row that rhymes with the first
One in the box

plate	bed	slate	kite
bag	sheep	yarn	tag
tank	bin	bank	gate
cake	snake	brain	hat
cook	mat	book	bat

Circle pictures that rhymes

Directions: Circle one picture in each row that rhymes with the first
One in the box

nut	penguin	igloo	cut
car	dam	jar	sheep
tap	cap	bin	juice
net	bat	cow	jet
hand	tree	wand	pit

Say True or False

Directions: Write ✓ or ✗ in the third column based on the phonics of first two columns

can	cab	✗
take	cake	✓
rub	tub	
lamp	lunch	
mob	food	
day	hay	
tip	truck	
god	rod	
sit	fit	
clog	job	
sack	back	
fog	shut	
cook	took	

Say True or False

Directions: Write ✓ or ✗ in the third column based on the phonics of first two columns

she	fee	
did	dad	
run	pod	
guest	best	
pet	get	
vat	fur	
cow	how	
far	net	
boy	girl	
crab	cab	
dip	spin	
bake	fig	
pop	hop	

Say True or False

Directions: Write ✓ or **X** in the third column based on the phonics of first two columns

bin	tin	
glide	bun	
wet	ram	
hot	pot	
fan	wand	
ship	he	
but	shut	
tank	bank	
fog	log	
toy	did	
rag	may	
win	sin	
late	slate	

Rhyming Bugs

Directions: Match the rhyming bugs. Color the two rhyming bugs using the same color.

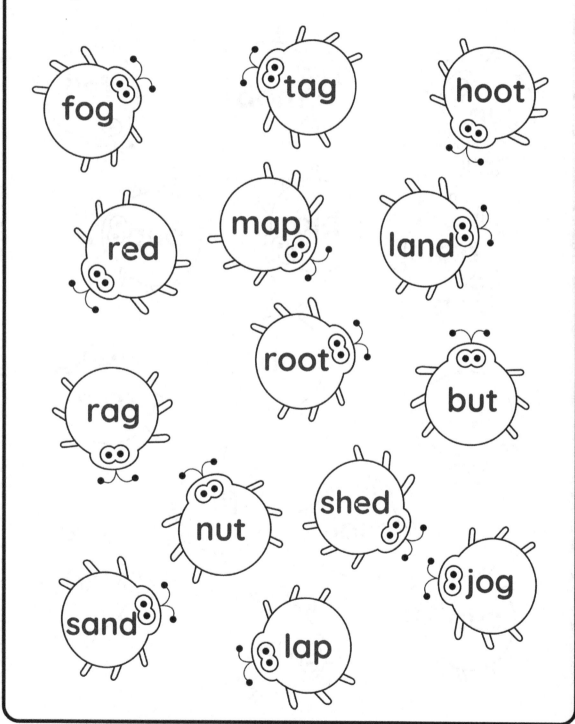

Rhyming Bugs

Directions: Match the rhyming bugs. Color the two rhyming bugs using the same color.

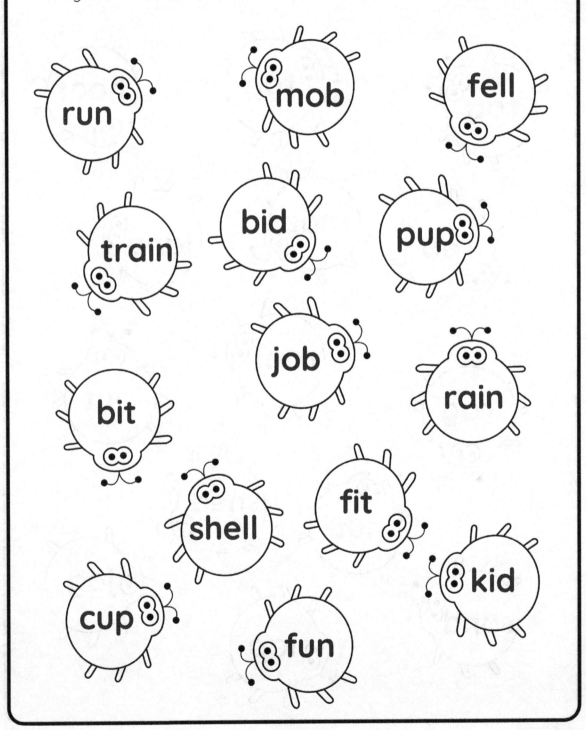

Rhyming Bugs

Directions: Match the rhyming bugs. Color the two rhyming bugs using the same color.

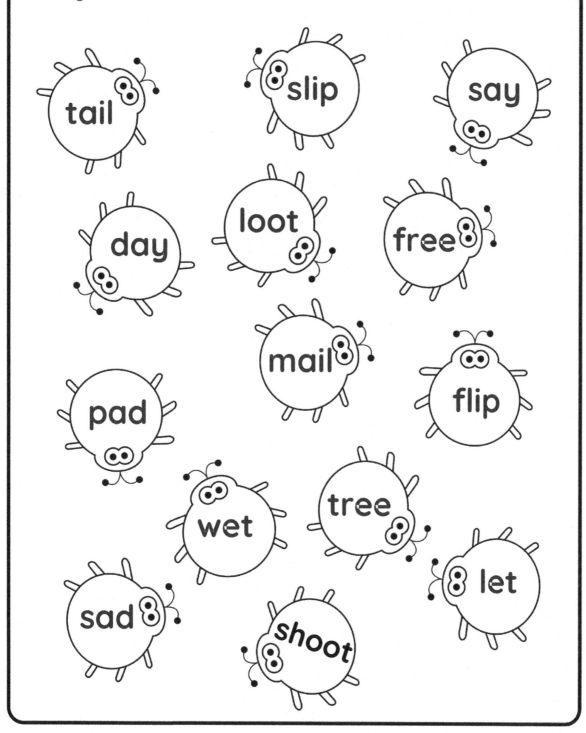

Color the Bubbles

Directions: Find the rhyming words in the bubbles below. Us the same color to fill in each set of bubbles that rhymes.

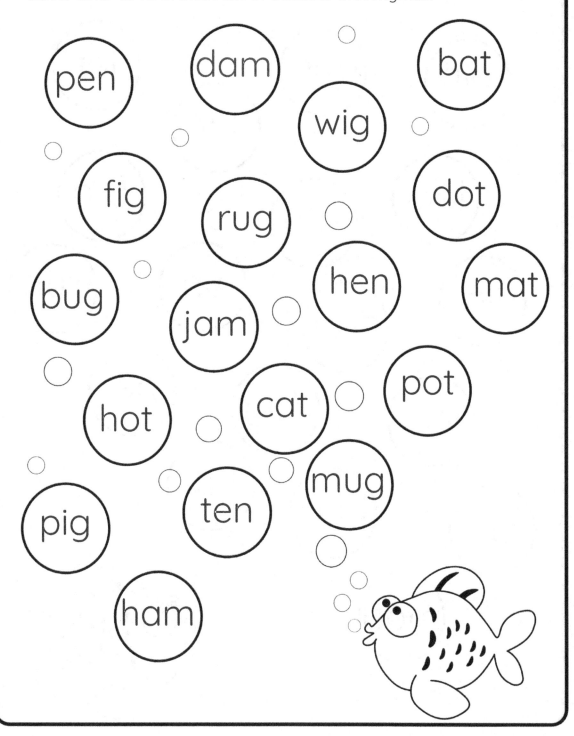

Color the Bubbles

Directions: Find the rhyming words in the bubbles below. Us the same color to fill in each set of bubbles that rhymes.

bin

pad

jet

hit

log

fog

sun

let

tin

run

dad

pet

win

dog

pit

sit

bun

mad

Color the Bubbles

Directions: Find the rhyming words in the bubbles below. Us the same color to fill in each set of bubbles that rhymes.

Circle the Rhyming Words

Directions: Circle the words in each row that rhymes with the first words

den	pet	men	pit	pun
wag	nag	big	win	tag
hug	hut	cat	mug	nab
can	ben	plan	ham	cot
met	mop	set	jet	blob
drop	dog	stop	pat	brag
smog	pop	mob	slam	log
nab	hay	crab	pit	nun
yam	yet	may	spam	log
sat	sit	pun	pat	cat
bit	jet	split	ben	pit
tub	tab	scrub	tin	cub
tip	nip	plot	rip	pit

Circle the Rhyming Words

Directions: Circle the words in each row that rhymes with the first words

got	plot	not	shed	run
nut	wig	gut	win	hut
bad	hut	lad	mug	nab
rob	rot	log	snob	quit
met	mop	set	jet	blob
fig	big	wig	fin	dig
pet	yet	plan	peg	win
bun	bug	nub	stun	ham
than	yet	fan	win	that
glad	yam	shut	dad	had
snob	grin	let	rob	bug
bed	wd	mug	red	bud
mat	pat	flat	boy	dip

Circle the Rhyming Words

Directions: Circle the words in each row that rhymes with the first words

globe	pin	road	hole	probe
cut	hut	sum	nut	took
hen	dog	when	light	ten
mouse	house	how	hit	tub
face	rat	gun	race	tell
make	ring	bake	case	box
parrot	mat	tin	carrot	tall
fish	nap	more	get	dish
box	fox	was	node	mole
float	wool	boat	look	kite
weed	four	lamp	seed	what
cave	tub	save	lawn	jar
dove	hop	goat	run	glove

Circle the Rhyming Words

Directions: Circle the words in each row that rhymes with the first words

top	log	cab	cop	woot
book	vat	fur	she	took
pot	fan	lot	fig	men
did	lid	she	hit	tub
get	fat	sack	wand	bet
rag	tag	put	free	mob
pet	shut	tick	pup	net
hug	yet	den	tug	crab
map	dad	nap	cop	ring
say	rod	mow	nod	pay
sing	wing	top	bit	that
sip	dot	fig	lip	sheep
bag	cup	tag	log	car

Circle the Rhyming Words

Directions: Circle the words in each row that rhymes with the first words

how	fly	cow	top	now
wet	let	fur	set	took
jump	go	bump	far	lump
day	hay	stay	hot	rub
wit	fat	dog	hit	sit
light	sight	fight	look	road
plan	shed	can	pup	van
well	sell	toy	tell	cab
grip	cat	dip	sale	lip
hole	fin	mole	role	den
big	tall	bed	fig	dig
cave	dot	save	lip	gave
cook	look	net	foot	hook

Write your own rhyming word

Directions: For each given word, write a list of words that rhyme with it.

car

1. _____
2. _____
3. _____

bee

1. _____
2. _____
3. _____

house

1. _____
2. _____
3. _____

key

1. _____
2. _____
3. _____

Write your own rhyming word

Directions: For each given word, write a list of words that rhyme with it.

tree

1. _____
2. _____
3. _____

hen

1. _____
2. _____
3. _____

bun

1. _____
2. _____
3. _____

snail

1. _____
2. _____
3. _____

Write your own rhyming word

Directions: For each given word, write a list of words that rhyme with it.

pin

1. _____
2. _____
3. _____

can

1. _____
2. _____
3. _____

boat

1. _____
2. _____
3. _____

dice

1. _____
2. _____
3. _____

Write your own rhyming word

Directions: For each given word, write a list of words that rhyme with it.

crab

1. _____
2. _____
3. _____

map

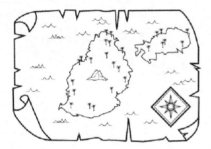

1. _____
2. _____
3. _____

wand

1. _____
2. _____
3. _____

lip

1. _____
2. _____
3. _____

Write your own rhyming word

Directions: For each given word, write a list of words that rhyme with it.

lamp

1. _____
2. _____
3. _____

juice

1. _____
2. _____
3. _____

pan

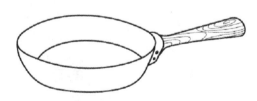

1. _____
2. _____
3. _____

book

1. _____
2. _____
3. _____

Write your own rhyming word

Directions: For each given word, write a list of words that rhyme with it.

sun

1. _____
2. _____
3. _____

hay

1. _____
2. _____
3. _____

bed

1. _____
2. _____
3. _____

nut

1. _____
2. _____
3. _____

Write your own rhyming word

Directions: For each given word, write a list of words that rhyme with it.

jar

1. _____
2. _____
3. _____

kite

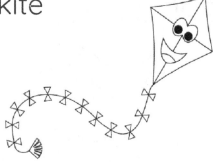

1. _____
2. _____
3. _____

bat

1. _____
2. _____
3. _____

ham

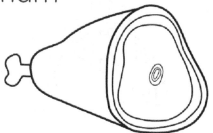

1. _____
2. _____
3. _____

Write your own rhyming word

Directions: For each given word, write a list of words that rhyme with it.

pad

1. _____
2. _____
3. _____

bag

1. _____
2. _____
3. _____

net
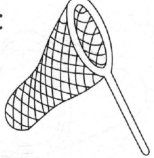

1. _____
2. _____
3. _____

pig

1. _____
2. _____
3. _____

Write your own rhyming word

Directions: For each given word, write a list of words that rhyme with it.

pit

1. _____
2. _____
3. _____

dog

1. _____
2. _____
3. _____

bug

1. _____
2. _____
3. _____

pot

1. _____
2. _____
3. _____

Rhyming Stories

Directions: Complete the rhyme so that it matches the picture.

Look at the _____

who is cutting a

_____

This little _____

is wearing a

_____

A _____

is sitting on a

_____

Rhyming Stories

Directions: Complete the rhyme so that it matches the picture.

Do you see an

_____

wearing a

_____

I see a _____

making a

_____

I see a _____

riding a _____

Rhyming Stories

Directions: Complete the rhyme so that it matches the picture.

Wearing a

_____, a

_____ is

sailing on a

_____

_____ in a

_____ is

wearing a pair of

_____

Big _____ wears a

_____, dances a

_____ with a

_____